The

SLIME

Workshop

20 DIY PROJECTS TO MAKE AWESOME SLIME

· · · · · · · · ·

ALL BORAX-FREE!

The SLIME Workshop

by

SELINA ZHANG

(@anathemaslime)

LARK
New York

LARK
New York

An Imprint of Sterling Publishing Co., Inc.
1166 Avenue of the Americas
New York, NY 10036

This publication is intended for informational purposes only. This publication is a guide to making variations
of slime and is intended for young readers with adult supervision. This publication includes DIY science
projects that contain everyday household ingredients that may cause minor reactions or trigger sensitivities
by contact or smelling. The projects in this publication are not recipes and do not produce food or edible items
in any respect. The slimes are fun and creative but are not intended to be eaten and certainly are not tasty,
so please Do Not Eat any of the ingredients or any slimes made from the projects in this publication. The publisher
shall not be liable or responsible in any respect for any use or application of any information contained in this
publication or any adverse effects, consequences, losses, or damages of any type resulting or arising from, directly
or indirectly, the use or application of any information contained in this publication. Any trademarks are the
property of their respective owners, are used for editorial purposes only, and do not indicate or suggest
a connection, endorsement, or association, and the publisher makes no claim of ownership and shall acquire
no right, title, or interest in such trademarks by virtue of this publication.

ISBN 978-1-4547-1066-0

Distributed in Canada by Sterling Publishing Co., Inc.
c/o Canadian Manda Group, 664 Annette Street
Toronto, Ontario, M6S 2C8, Canada
Distributed in the United Kingdom by GMC Distribution Services
Castle Place, 166 High Street, Lewes, East Sussex, BN7 1XU, England
Distributed in Australia by NewSouth Books
45 Beach Street, Coogee, NSW 2034, Australia

For information about custom editions, special sales, and premium and corporate purchases, please contact Sterling
Special Sales at 800-805-5489 or specialsales@sterlingpublishing.com.

Manufactured in Canada

Lot #:
8 10 9 7
01/19

sterlingpublishing.com
larkcrafts.com

Interior Design by Shannon Nicole Plunkett

For my mom

Contents

Letter from Selina

Welcome to *The Slime Workshop*! In this book, there are 20 different projects to make super-fun and super-awesome slimes. They range from glossy to matte, crunchy, and more! I first stumbled upon these different slimes when I was 13 years old, and they instantly drew me in. The first slime that I ever made was a white fluffy slime. After that, I couldn't wait to experiment with different slimes. I love how pretty they can look and how they help me unwind, especially after a busy day at school.

I started a small slime account on Instagram in October 2016, and since then it's grown to more than 350,000 followers! A few months later, I created my own website: anathemaslime.com. My first Instagram post was a badly filmed fluffy slime on a chair; at the time, I thought it was a great video but now . . . not so much. Luckily, I've gotten much better at filming videos! I upload new slime photos and videos on my website and Instagram whenever I have free time. It's been a blast showing the slimes I've made to my followers online, and I can't wait to share the slime projects in this book with you! Making and playing with slime has been so fun and relaxing for me. Now you can discover the fun of making these slimes all on your own. I hope you enjoy reading this book as much as I enjoyed writing it!

-Selina

Introduction

What's not to love about slime? Reasons why slime is awesome:

- You can make it with ordinary ingredients you probably already have at home.

- It's super-fun to stretch, poke, pull, fold, and knead.

- You can make it shiny, colorful, metallic, matte, glittery, crunchy, glossy, or sandy.

- There are endless ways to experiment with different textures and sounds.

- You can even make it inflate!

The Slime Workshop contains all the information you need to create your own slime laboratory at home. These twenty projects are not only a fun introduction to slime-making for a new slime maker, but they also contain variations and tips that even an experienced slime maker will find eye-opening and fun!

If you're looking for a slime that is super-stretchy and shiny, then Glossy Slime is the one for you. Want something with crunch? Fishbowl Slime is your answer. Need a slime that pops when you squeeze it? Foam slime is what you're after. Looking for some sizzle with your slime? Bubbly Slime will scratch that itch.

Flip through the Getting Started section to see what tools and materials you'll need, how to troubleshoot your slime, and learn about the science behind the goo if you're curious.

So gather your supplies, pick your workstation, and get sliming!

Getting Started

The Science of Slime

What is slime? To answer that question, first we need to talk about Sir Isaac Newton. Newton is one of the most influential scientists of all time and lived in England in the 17th century. You might know him best from the story of how an apple falling from a tree led him to the discovery of gravity. While that may be one of his most important discoveries, he also spent a lot of time studying fluids.

Newton observed that the viscosity of a fluid—how fast or slow it flows—is affected by temperature. Fluids that are hot flow quickly, and fluids that are cold flow slowly. Cold maple syrup pours more slowly than hot maple syrup. But what if a fluid *doesn't* react to temperature? These are called non-Newtonian fluids, and they don't obey the same rules of viscosity. Slime is an example of a non-Newtonian fluid.

If temperature doesn't affect the viscosity of non-Newtonian fluids like slime, what does? The answer is applying "shear stress," like pulling, squishing, and stirring. Does this sound familiar? It's exactly what you do to mix up slime! Pulling, squishing, and stirring cause slime to thicken.

So how does mixing glue with other ingredients create slime? Glue is a polymer—a long chain of repeating molecules. Liquid starch is also a polymer. When these two highly viscous polymers come together, a process called cross-linking occurs. Bonds are formed, and they link together these long chains of molecules. By doing so, a viscous liquid becomes that stuff we know and love—slime!

What Is a Slime Activator?

A slime activator is the liquid ingredient that binds your mixture together to create that slimy consistency. In *The Slime Workshop,* we'll be using two different activators:

- Liquid starch
- Contact lens solution with diluted baking soda (see below)

For most slimes, liquid starch can be used interchangeably with the combination of contact lens solution and diluted baking soda.

If you are using contact lens solution, make sure it contains boric acid. Combining contact lens solution that contains boric acid with baking soda creates borate ions. When mixed with glue, these ions are responsible for the cross-linking that will create slime.

To make the diluted baking soda, combine 2 teaspoons (10 ml) baking soda with ½ cup (118 ml) hot water (**ask an adult to help you heat the water**), and mix until dissolved. Alternate between pouring a teaspoon of the diluted baking soda and a teaspoon of contact lens solution into the slime.

Slime Safety

Making slime is fun, but it's important to remember that slime-making is a science. Before you get started on these craft-meets-chemistry projects, it's important to observe some basic safety precautions.

IT'S CHEMISTRY!

This is science, so the basic rules of a science experiment apply to slime-making: **Never** eat the ingredients you use to make slime or the slime itself, and **never** rub your eyes until after you've properly washed your hands.

HAND-WASHING

It's **very important** to wash your hands before **and especially after** handling any of the ingredients. Having clean hands before you begin mixing slime ensures that you don't add anything from your hands into your slime. (No one wants dirt or sandwich crumbs in their slime, right?) Having clean hands after you mix slime also ensures that you don't accidentally swallow these chemicals. Speaking of which . . .

WASHING TOOLS

You'll be using mixing bowls, liquid-measuring cups, measuring spoons, and other tools that will likely come from your kitchen. It's best to have tools that you use only for slime. To clean your tools, rinse them under running water, wash them using a sponge and a squirt of dish soap, and then rinse and dry. You don't want a side of slime with your meatloaf!

* ASK YOUR PARENTS! *

Always make sure you ask an adult for permission before you get started. **Make sure they always supervise you**, too. Especially have an adult nearby if you're making the Candle Slime, Foam Slime, Fishbowl Slime, Bubble-Bath Slime, and Bubblegum Slime. These slimes use materials that require supervision so you can stay safe.

Your Slime-Making Tool Kit

Before you get started on slime-making, you'll need to assemble your Slime-Making Tool Kit. This tool kit contains the tools and materials you need to get started on any project in this book.

BOWL

You can use a mixing bowl, a salad bowl, or any deep container for mixing slime. This bowl is what you'll use to pour your ingredients into and stir and knead your slime.

STIRRING UTENSIL

A spoon, a chopstick, a craft stick, or even a pen could work as your stirring utensil. If you're planning to double or triple the projects in this book to make big batches of slime, you'll want to look for a larger stirring utensil, such as a paint-mixing stick, a long-handled spoon, or a spatula.

LIQUID-MEASURING CUP

This clear cup has measurement markings along its side to allow you to measure liquid in volume. Measurements are in ounces and milliliters. A liquid-measuring cup with a measurement of at least 8 ounces (237 ml) will work for these projects.

MEASURING SPOONS

Measuring spoons are used to measure the volume of dry ingredients and typically come in a set ranging from ¼ teaspoon to 1 tablespoon. For these projects, you'll only need the 1-teaspoon and 1-tablespoon measuring spoons.

SLIME ACTIVATOR

Both contact lens solution used with the diluted baking soda and liquid starch can be used interchangeably as slime activators for most projects in this book, so the choice of activator is yours.

AIRTIGHT CONTAINER

To make your slime last longer, you have to properly store it so it doesn't dry out, harden, or get dirty. Be sure to have an 8- to 12-ounce (237- to 355-ml) airtight container to immediately store your slime in as soon as you're finished playing with it.

Materials

Here's an overview of all the materials you'll be using in the projects. For help finding certain ingredients, take a look at the Resources section (page 73).

PVA GLUE

This is your basic glue that comes in two varieties: white glue and clear glue. PVA glue can conveniently be found in small bottles (handy for taking to school) as well as gallon jugs. The white glue is what you'll use for an opaque slime, and the clear glue is what you'll need for clear slimes. If you plan on making a lot of slime, it's a good idea to invest in the gallon-size jugs of glue.

SLIME ACTIVATORS

As mentioned earlier, these are the liquid ingredients that bind your mixtures together to create slime. They are:

— Liquid starch

Liquid starch is great to use when ironing to get crisp collars on your shirts or when you want to activate your slime! This can be found in big-box stores.

— Contact lens solution

Dirty contacts? Swish them around in some contact lens solution. Your slime needs activating? Mix this in! Contact lens solution is easily available at most drugstores, but make sure yours has boric acid as an ingredient!

— Baking soda

Scientifically known as sodium bicarbonate, baking soda is a fine white powder that has a wide variety of uses, including cooking, cleaning, and even pest control. Baking soda is an important component of the contact lens solution and diluted baking soda slime activator. Be sure to check the expiration of your baking soda. It can be less effective past the expiration date and impact the cross-linking in your slime.

Your Slime Workstation

Making slime is a sticky business, so choose your workstation carefully. Look for a smooth surface like a table or desk and avoid getting your slime ingredients—and, later, your fully formed slime—in contact with fabric or upholstered items like your clothes, couch, or rug. You can use your kitchen counter, but be sure to clean the surface with a disinfectant wipe or a rag and all-purpose cleaner after each use since this is a surface where food is prepared. To protect your surfaces and make cleanup easy, lay down a large square of wax paper, a plastic place mat, or a plastic tablecloth on top of your workstation. Avoid using newspaper or regular paper—these might stick to your slime.

SHAVING CREAM

Shaving cream helps give fluffy slimes their fluffy consistency. You'll want to use the foaming shaving creams (not the gels).

FOAMING HAND SOAP

Foaming hand soap helps make fluffy slimes even fluffier. Make sure you get *foaming* hand soap, not regular hand soap, since it's the foam that's crucial for a fluffy slime.

FOAMING FACE WASH

Foaming face wash also helps make fluffy slimes even fluffier. Again, make sure you get a *foaming* face wash, not just any face wash, since the foam is key for fluffiness.

LOTION

Lotion helps make your slime stretchier. Any lotion will work, and you probably already have some lying around at home. Use a scented lotion to add a pleasant aroma to your slime.

MODELING CLAY

When making butter slimes, modeling clay is what gives this slime its spreadable, opaque, and smooth, butter-like consistency. Modeling clay dries out when exposed to air, so be sure to store this clay in an airtight container when not in use.

CORNSTARCH-BASED BABY POWDER

This can be substituted for cornstarch in the Matte Slime (page 49). The baby powder gives a matte appearance to the slime, and the cornstarch in the baby powder helps thicken it.

GLITTER

Add a little bling to your slime with some glitter! There are a variety of glitter textures and colors you can buy—from fine glitter and larger glitter pieces to fun glitter shapes. Experiment with colors and types to create some eye-catching slime.

CRAFT FOAM BEADS OR POLYSTYRENE BALLS

These tiny foam beads are an important ingredient when making Foam Slime (page 59). The texture of polystyrene balls is what gives this type of slime that satisfying *crunch* sound each time you smash or stretch it.

FOOD COLORING

Food coloring is a colored liquid that comes in tiny bottles and can be found in any store or supermarket, in the baking aisle. Add just one drop at a time since a little goes a long way.

PIGMENT

Pigments add color to your slime and look like very fine, flour-like powder. They produce a vivid color and are also available in metallic shades to make metallic slimes. You'll want to be careful when working with pigment, since it can easily fly everywhere and stain your clothes, carpet, and other surfaces.

PAINT

Paint is a much less expensive—and more easily available—alternative to pigments when coloring slime. Acrylic paints are widely available at any craft store in an array of colors and even come in metallic shades if you want to add a little shimmer to the slime.

Coloring Slime

You can add color to slime using food coloring, pigment, or paint when you begin mixing your first ingredients together or after you've added your activator and are happy with the slime's texture and consistency. Most of the instructions will tell you to add color at the beginning. This will help you keep your hands cleaner, but you can save the coloring for later, too.

If you want to add your coloring after your slime is fully formed, then you'll find that mixing slime with your coloring of choice is very similar to kneading dough. You will:

• Place the slime on a clean surface. Add drops of food coloring, paint, or a few sprinkles of pigment to the center of your slime.

• Grab a piece of slime from its outer edge, stretch it out, fold it toward the center of the slime, and poke through the slime with your fingers. Repeat this stretch, fold, and poke technique all around the circumference of the slime. This process will contain the color inside the slime so it doesn't leak out before you've had a chance to mix it.

• Pick up your slime, hold one half in each hand, pull your hands apart to stretch the slime, fold it in half, and then stretch the slime again. Repeat a few times to get the food coloring, paint, or pigment to fully combine with the slime.

• Place the slime back on the clean surface and start the stretch, fold, and poke technique again. Repeat until you're satisfied with the color and its distribution throughout the slime.

GLOW-IN-THE-DARK POWDER

This is also called phosphorescent powder and will make your slime glow in the dark. When you mix this powder with your slime, you just need to let the slime "charge" under natural light or any light source, then turn out the lights and watch it glow!

CLEAR MINI ACRYLIC VASE FILLERS

Vase filler is used for fishbowl slimes and to give slimes a fun *crunch* when playing with them. They are tiny beads used decoratively inside vases. If you're having trouble finding vase filler, you can also use seed beads or pony beads. All of these beads can be found at most craft stores.

FAKE SNOW POWDER

Add a little water to this powder and watch it instantly grow into fake, fluffy snow. Mix it up in the Snowball Slime (page 53) and you can make a snowman any time of the year!

WATER BEADS

Water beads look like tiny, hard, round seeds when they're dry. When you soak them in water, they grow several times larger and feel like squishy, slippery pearls. Crush them up for a jiggly Bubble-Bath Slime (page 57).

SAND

Sand can be found at hardware stores as play sand for backyard sandboxes, as well as at craft stores in a variety of colors for sand-art crafts. If you buy colored art sand, you won't need to color your Sand Slime (page 39).

CANDLES

Wax shavings from candles give the Candle Slime (page 40) a soft and waxy texture. Use a scented candle to make scented slime! Use caution when handling hot wax and **make sure you have adult supervision**.

PACKING PEANUTS

Who knew that packing peanuts could both protect your fragile items in the mail *and* be crushed to resemble chewed bubblegum in the Bubblegum Slime (page 37)? If you don't have packing peanuts, you can work with any piece of foam and break it up into small pieces.

TISSUES

When you're making the Papier-Mâché Slime (page 67), tissues can be used to mimic the lumpy strips of paper in traditional papier-mâché crafting. Since tissues are very soft and easily break down, the more you work this slime, the more the tissues disintegrate into it.

Oops! Getting the Slime Out

Did that slime have a mind of its own and get all over you, the rug, and the couch? Accidents happen, but vinegar is a miracle cure for slime cleanup.

- **SLIME IN YOUR HAIR:** For long hair, pour vinegar into a bowl and dip the slime-covered hair into the bowl. Let it soak for one minute and then use your fingers to pull the slime out. Once all the slime is out, throw away the vinegar and shampoo the hair. For short hair or slime that's near the scalp, soak a washcloth with vinegar and then apply the wet washcloth to the slime. Be careful not to let the vinegar drip into your eyes! After a minute of soaking the hair with the vinegar washcloth, use your fingers to remove the slime from the hair. Once it's all out, shampoo the hair and launder the washcloth.

- **SLIME ON THE CARPET:** Use a spoon to scrape up all the excess slime. Work from the outer edges of the slime toward the center to avoid spreading it. Once all the excess is scraped up, pour enough vinegar over the remaining slime in the carpet to saturate the spot. Wait one minute and then use a clean spoon to scrape up the remainder of the slime. Blot the spot with a clean cloth dampened with water. Once the area is dry, vacuum that spot in the carpet.

- **SLIME ON YOUR CLOTHES:** Lay the article of clothing down on a smooth surface and use a spoon to scrape up all the extra slime, working from the outer edges to the center to avoid creating a larger slime stain. Once you have removed as much as you can, pour vinegar over the remaining slime to soak the spot. Wait one minute and then use a clean spoon to scrape up the remainder of the slime. Rinse the clothing in warm water and then launder as you normally would.

- **SLIME ON THE COUCH (or other upholstered surface):** Use a spoon to scrape up all the excess slime. Work from the outer edges of the slime toward the center to avoid creating a larger slime stain. Once all the excess slime is scraped up, pour enough vinegar over the remaining slime on the couch to saturate the spot. Wait one minute and then use a clean spoon to scrape up the remainder of the slime. Blot the spot with a clean cloth dampened with water.

Storing Your Slime

When you're finished playing with slime, you should always store it in an 8- to 12-ounce (237- to 355-ml) airtight container. Plastic food containers are great for storing slime and can be found at most stores in the same section as sandwich bags and aluminum foil. Or you can reuse the plastic containers from last night's takeout.

Troubleshooting Your Slime

Having some trouble with your slime? While slime is a science, it can also be a finicky art and require tweaking to get the just-right slime consistency. Here are some common problems when making slime and how to solve them.

SLIME IS DRIED OUT

If your slime is feeling a little dry, you just need to give it a little moisture for it to bounce back. You can either add some lotion or run it under warm water. Unfortunately, Butter Slime (page 50) cannot be fixed once it's dried out. Butter Slime is made with modeling clay, and once the clay hardens, the slime hardens. You'll need to make a new batch.

SLIME IS TOO HARD AND BREAKS

If your slime is too hard to play with and rips or breaks when you pull it apart, then you need to soften it. Soften slime made with white PVA glue by adding some lotion. Add a few pumps, then stretch the slime to mix it in. Keep adding more lotion to soften it up until you achieve a consistency that you like. You can soften slime made with clear PVA glue by running it under warm water.

SLIME IS TOO STICKY

If your slime is sticking to your fingers when you play with it, then you just need to add more slime activator. Add a few drops at a time and work it into the slime until your slime stops sticking to your fingers or the bowl.

BEADS ARE FALLING OUT

If beads are falling out of your slime, then you either have too many beads in the slime or the slime is too stiff. Just add a little bit more slime a ½ ounce (15 ml) at a time until the beads stop falling out. You can also try softening up your slime with some lotion to help the beads stay in. Be careful not to use too much activator. The slime should be a little sticky in order for the beads to stay in.

Know When It's Time to Throw Out Your Slime

All good things must come to an end, right? Well, slime doesn't last forever. You'll know that it's time to throw out your slime when:

- It has a funny odor.
- The color has changed dramatically.
- It's not working properly and not responding to any of the troubleshooting tips you've tried.

Are you ready to make some slime? Jump in!

SLIME
Projects

Glossy Slime!

This is a shiny slime that is fun to poke, stretch, and squeeze. It is a basic slime that the other projects in this book are built on and is a great starting point for experimenting with your own original slimes.

WHAT YOU'LL NEED

Slime-Making Tool Kit

8 ounces (237 ml) white PVA glue

1 tablespoon (15 ml) lotion

your choice of food coloring, pigment, or paint in any color

activator: 6 tablespoons (89 ml) liquid starch OR 3 teaspoons (15 ml) contact lens solution and 2 teaspoons (10 ml) diluted baking soda (see page 11)

WHAT YOU'LL DO

1. Pour the white PVA glue, lotion, and coloring ingredient into a bowl.

2. Using your stirring utensil, mix these ingredients together.

3. Pour in 1 tablespoon (15 ml) of liquid starch or 1 teaspoon (5 ml) each of diluted baking soda and contact lens solution.

4. Using your stirring utensil, mix the activator into the ingredients.

5. Repeat Steps 3 and 4 until the slime pulls away from the bowl. If the slime still looks too runny, try adding a few more drops of liquid starch, or alternate between adding a few drops of diluted baking soda and a few drops of contact lens solution until it thickens.

6. Knead the mixture with either the stirring utensil or your hands.

7. Add drops of liquid starch or contact lens solution a little bit at a time until the slime is not sticky. The slime should feel slippery, soft, and stretchy and should not stick to your fingers.

8. Enjoy your slime, and remember to store it in an airtight container when you're finished.

Milky Slime

Here's a thinner and glossier alternative to Glossy Slime.

WHAT ELSE YOU'LL NEED

1 tablespoon (15 ml) baby oil

2–3 ounces (60–88 ml) water

WHAT YOU'LL DO

1. Pour the white PVA glue, lotion, coloring ingredient, baby oil, and water into a bowl.

2. Using your stirring utensil, mix these ingredients together.

3. Follow Steps 3 through 8 of the Glossy Slime (page 25).

Wow!

Jiggly Slime

This is a glossy slime with a twist—it jiggles and bounces every time you play with it.

WHAT YOU'LL NEED

Slime-Making Tool Kit

8 ounces (237 ml) white PVA glue

1 tablespoon (15 ml) lotion

your choice of food coloring, pigment, or paint in any color

6 ounces (177 ml) water

activator: 6 tablespoons (89 ml) liquid starch OR 3 teaspoons (15 ml) contact lens solution and 2 teaspoons (10 ml) diluted baking soda (see page 11)

Tips

• The more water you add, the jigglier the slime will be.

• Try this with clear PVA glue! You will end up with a jelly-like clear slime. Just be sure to use more activator (see page 43 for amounts).

WHAT YOU'LL DO

1. Pour the white PVA glue, lotion, and coloring ingredient into a bowl.

2. Using your stirring utensil, mix these ingredients together.

3. Gradually add the water to the bowl while stirring with the mixing utensil. Be careful not to spill the water while mixing.

4. Pour in 1 tablespoon (15 ml) of liquid starch or 1 teaspoon (5 ml) each of diluted baking soda and contact lens solution.

5. Using your stirring utensil, mix the activator into the ingredients.

6. Repeat Steps 4 and 5 until the slime pulls away from the bowl. If the slime still looks too runny, try adding a few more drops of liquid starch or alternate between adding a few drops of diluted baking soda and a few drops of contact lens solution until it thickens.

7. Knead the mixture with either the stirring utensil or your hands.

8. Add drops of liquid starch or contact lens solution a little bit at a time until the slime is not sticky. The slime will feel watery and slippery, but you should be able to hold it in your hands.

9. Enjoy your slime, and remember to store it in an airtight container when you're finished.

Glitter-Bomb Slime

This crunchy, crackly, glitter-filled slime can be holographic, metallic, and all sorts of rainbow colors!

WHAT YOU'LL NEED

Slime-Making Tool Kit

4 ounces (118 ml) clear PVA glue

activator: 6 tablespoons (89 ml) liquid starch OR 5 teaspoons (25 ml) contact lens solution and 4 teaspoons (20 ml) diluted baking soda (see page 11)

bowl (separate from what's in your usual Tool Kit)

1 cup (236 g) glitter in any color

WHAT YOU'LL DO

1. Pour the clear PVA glue into a bowl.

2. Pour in 1 tablespoon (15 ml) of liquid starch or 1 teaspoon (5 ml) each of diluted baking soda and contact lens solution.

3. Using your stirring utensil, mix the activator into the glue.

4. Repeat Steps 2 and 3 until the slime pulls away from bowl. The slime should be slightly sticky so it can hold in the glitter. If the slime still looks too runny, try adding a few more drops of liquid starch, or alternate between adding a few drops of diluted baking soda and a few drops of contact lens solution until it thickens.

5. Knead the slime mixture until the activator is fully combined into the slime.

6. Pour the glitter into a second bowl.

7. Dip the slime in the bowl of glitter. Knead the slime to mix in the glitter.

8. Repeat Step 7 as many times as you want. Make sure you don't add more than 3 times the amount of glitter to the slime, or the glitter may fall out.

9. Enjoy your slime, and remember to store it in an airtight container when you're finished.

Tip

If the glitter is sticking to your hands, the slime may be too sticky. Mix in a few extra drops of liquid starch or contact lens solution.

Unicorn Slime

Make a slime as legendary as the unicorn. Mixing five colors of slime together creates a magical, marbled effect!

WHAT YOU'LL NEED

Slime-Making Tool Kit

8 ounces (237 ml) white PVA glue

1 tablespoon (15 ml) lotion

activator: 6 tablespoons (89 ml) liquid starch OR 3 teaspoons (15 ml) contact lens solution and 2 teaspoons (10 ml) diluted baking soda (see page 11)

your choice of food coloring, pigment, or paint in blue, pink, yellow, green, and purple

glitter: iridescent or holographic silver (optional)

WHAT YOU'LL DO

1. Pour the white PVA glue and lotion into a bowl. Using your stirring utensil, mix these ingredients together.

2. Pour in 1 tablespoon (15 ml) of liquid starch or 1 teaspoon (5 ml) each of diluted baking soda and contact lens solution.

3. Using your stirring utensil, mix the activator into the ingredients. Repeat Step 2 until the slime pulls away from the bowl. If the slime still looks too runny, try adding a few more drops of liquid starch, or alternate between adding a few drops of diluted baking soda and a few drops of contact lens solution until it thickens.

4. Knead the mixture with either the stirring utensil or your hands.

5. Add drops of liquid starch or contact lens solution a little bit at a time until the slime is not sticky. The slime should feel slippery, soft, and stretchy.

6. Divide the slime into five equal parts.

7. Pour the blue coloring ingredient on one part of the slime, pink on the second part of slime, yellow on the third part of slime, green on the fourth part of slime, and purple on the last part of slime.

8. Knead each color of slime separately, using your stirring utensil to fully mix in the color.

9. Swirl all five colors together to create a marbled effect. (See the next page for details on how to create marbled slime.)

10. If you want to add glitter, place the marbled slime in a bowl and sprinkle glitter onto the slime. Add as much glitter as you want, but make sure not to put more than 1 ounce (28 g) of glitter for every 3 ounces (85 g) of slime or the glitter may fall out.

11. Enjoy your slime, and remember to store it in an airtight container when you're finished.

How to:
Marble Your Slime

To make marbled slime, hold all the different colored slimes in both hands, then stretch the slimes, fold and twist them, and repeat until you're satisfied with the marbled effect.

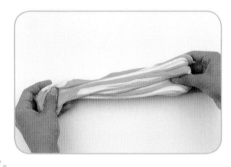

Try this!

Rainbow Slime

Make a rainbow slime using the same instructions! Instead of unicorn colors, use the colors of the rainbow with some iridescent sprinkles to create something that looks out of this world.

Blow slowly into the straw so the bubble doesn't pop too fast!

WARNING

This slime uses packing peanuts, which pose a potential choking hazard. Make sure an adult is supervising, especially if you're blowing bubbles in the slime with a straw!

Bubblegum Slime

This chunky slime with a glossy base resembles chewed-up bubblegum. It might look real enough to chew, but **this slime is definitely not for eating!**

WHAT YOU'LL NEED

Slime-Making Tool Kit

8 ounces (237 ml) white PVA glue

1 tablespoon (15 ml) lotion

your choice of food coloring, pigment, or paint in any color

activator: 6 tablespoons (89 ml) liquid starch OR 3 teaspoons (15 ml) contact lens solution and 2 teaspoons (10 ml) diluted baking soda diluted baking soda (see page 11)

5–10 packing peanuts

Tips

• Use pink food coloring, paint, or pigment to make your slime look like actual bubblegum!

• If you don't have packing peanuts, take a piece of polystyrene foam, which is usually found in shipping packages, and break it up into little chunks.

WHAT YOU'LL DO

1. Pour the white PVA glue, lotion, and coloring ingredient into a bowl. Using your stirring utensil, mix these ingredients together.

2. Pour in 1 tablespoon (15 ml) of liquid starch or 1 teaspoon (5 ml) each of diluted baking soda and contact lens solution.

3. Using your stirring utensil, mix the activator into the ingredients.

4. Repeat Steps 2 and 3 until the slime pulls away from the bowl. If the slime still looks too runny, try adding a few more drops of liquid starch, or alternate between adding a few drops of diluted baking soda and a few drops of contact lens solution until it thickens.

5. Knead the mixture with either the stirring utensil or your hands.

6. Add drops of liquid starch or contact lens solution a little bit at a time until the slime is not sticky. The slime should feel slippery, soft, and stretchy.

7. Sprinkle the packing peanuts on top of the slime.

8. Using your hands, knead the slime to combine the packing peanuts. They will break into pieces the more you play with the slime, making it look like chewed-up bubblegum.

Sand Slime

This textured slime is made with sand and can even hold its shape when you mold it.

WHAT YOU'LL NEED

Slime-Making Tool Kit

8 ounces (237 ml) white PVA glue

1 tablespoon (15 ml) lotion

your choice of food coloring, pigment, or paint in any color (optional)

1 cup (379 g) sand

activator: 6 tablespoons (89 ml) liquid starch OR 3 teaspoons (15 ml) contact lens solution and 2 teaspoons (10 ml) diluted baking soda (see page 11)

Tips

• Like with the Snowball Slime and Foam Slime, you can make fun shapes with Sand Slime. Get creative and try using cookie cutters!

• Don't add too much sand, or the slime may become too hard and not as stretchy. If there is too much sand, add more plain slime, teaspoon by teaspoon, until you're satisfied with the result.

WHAT YOU'LL DO

1. Pour the white PVA glue, lotion, and coloring ingredient into a bowl.

2. Using your stirring utensil, mix these ingredients together.

3. Pour in the sand. Use your hands to knead the mixture until the sand is fully combined.

4. Pour in 1 tablespoon (15 ml) of liquid starch or 1 teaspoon (5 ml) each of diluted baking soda and contact lens solution.

5. Knead the mixture with either the stirring utensil or your hands until the activator is fully combined.

6. Repeat Steps 4 and 5 until the slime pulls away from the bowl. If the slime still looks too runny, try adding a few more drops of liquid starch, or alternate between adding a few drops of diluted baking soda and a few drops of contact lens solution until it thickens.

7. Knead the slime with the stirring utensil or your hands.

8. Add drops of liquid starch or contact lens solution a little bit at a time until the slime is not sticky. The slime should feel textured and stretchy.

9. Enjoy your slime, and remember to store it in an airtight container when you're finished.

Candle Slime

This thick, fluffy slime is made with candles. It is super-soft and smooth and may feel a little waxy.

WHAT YOU'LL NEED

Slime-Making Tool Kit

spoon or butter knife

4 ounces (118 ml) candle wax

microwavable bowl

microwave

pot holder

8 ounces (237 ml) white PVA glue

activator: 6 tablespoons (89 ml) liquid starch OR 3 teaspoons (15 ml) contact lens solution and 2 teaspoons (10 ml) diluted baking soda (see page 11)

your choice of food coloring, pigment, or paint in any color

WARNING

This slime requires melting candle wax in a microwave. Use caution when handling the hot bowl and hot wax. Make sure an adult is supervising!

WHAT YOU'LL DO

1. Using the spoon or butter knife, scrape 4 ounces (118 ml) of wax from a candle and collect the shavings in a microwavable bowl.

2. Microwave the candle wax shavings for 60 seconds or until the wax has melted. Be sure to use a pot holder each time you pull the bowl out of the microwave—it may be hot.

3. Pour 4 ounces (118 ml) of the white PVA glue into the bowl of melted candle wax. Using your stirring utensil, mix the ingredients together.

4. Microwave the mixture again for 30–60 seconds, or until all the chunks are melted. Using your stirring utensil, mix the ingredients together.

5. Pour the remaining 4 ounces (118 ml) of white PVA glue into the bowl. Using your stirring utensil, mix the ingredients together.

6. Microwave the mixture one more time for 15–30 seconds, or until there are no chunks remaining.

7. Pour in 1 tablespoon (15 ml) of liquid starch or 1 teaspoon (5 ml) each of diluted baking soda and contact lens solution.

8. Using your stirring utensil, mix the activator into the bowl.

9. Repeat Steps 7 and 8 until the slime pulls away from the bowl. If the slime still looks too runny, try adding a few more drops of liquid starch, or alternate between adding a few drops of diluted baking soda and a few drops of contact lens solution until it thickens.

10. Pour the coloring ingredient onto the slime.

11. Knead the slime with the stirring utensil or your hands. If the slime is too hot to touch, let it cool down before you begin kneading.

12. Add drops of liquid starch or contact lens solution a little bit at a time until the slime is not sticky. The slime should feel soft, fluffy, and smooth.

13. Enjoy your slime, and remember to store it in an airtight container when you're finished.

Tip

Experiment with different scented candles! The scent of the candle will transfer to your slime, so pick your favorite. Mine are citrusy, clean scents.

Tip

Food coloring is the most common dye to use for slimes, but you can also substitute different materials such as paints or pigments! The best for fishbowl and other clear PVA glue–based slimes is food coloring, as it will keep the slime clear and the vase filler from falling out. Paint or pigment may cause the slime to be less sticky, which will make the filler beads fall out.

Fishbowl Slime

This is a crunchy, clear PVA glue–based slime that I invented. I named this "fishbowl slime" because the clear beads provide an extra "watery" crunch and because the beads themselves look like they would be used in a fishbowl.

WHAT YOU'LL NEED

Slime-Making Tool Kit

activator: 6 tablespoons (89 ml) liquid starch OR 5 teaspoons (25 ml) contact lens solution and 4 teaspoons (20 ml) diluted baking soda (see page 11)

4 ounces (118 ml) clear PVA glue

your choice of food coloring, pigment or paint in any color

bowl (separate from what's in your usual Tool Kit)

1 cup (236 g) clear mini acrylic vase filler

WARNING

This slime uses acrylic vase filler, which poses a potential choking hazard. Make sure an adult is supervising!

WHAT YOU'LL DO

1. Pour the clear PVA glue and coloring ingredient into a bowl.

2. Pour in 1 tablespoon (15 ml) of liquid starch or 1 teaspoon (5 ml) each of diluted baking soda and contact lens solution. Using your stirring utensil, mix the activator into the ingredients.

3. Repeat Step 2 until the slime pulls away from the bowl. The slime should be a little sticky so that it holds in the clear mini acrylic vase filler. If the slime still looks too runny, add a few more drops of liquid starch, or alternate between adding a few drops of diluted baking soda and a few drops of contact lens solution until it thickens.

4. Knead the mixture with either the stirring utensil or your hands until the activator is fully combined into the slime.

5. Pour the vase filler into a separate bowl.

6. Dip the slime in the bowl of vase filler to get it to stick to the slime. Knead the slime to mix it in.

7. Repeat Step 6 as many times as you want. The more vase filler you mix into the slime, the crunchier the slime will be. Be careful not to add too much vase filler. Use a maximum ratio of 3 parts vase filler to 1 part slime; otherwise the filler may fall out.

8. Enjoy your slime, and remember to store it in an airtight container when you're finished.

Clear Slime

Clear slime has a different texture than white PVA glue-based slimes. It can be very clear if made correctly. If you need some help, see the next page!

WHAT YOU'LL NEED

Slime-Making Tool Kit

8 ounces (237 ml) clear PVA glue

activator: 5 teaspoons (25 ml) contact lens solution and 4 teaspoons (20 ml) diluted baking soda (see page 11)

WARNING

If you add beads to the slime, remember that they pose a potential choking hazard. Make sure an adult is supervising!

WHAT YOU'LL DO

1. Pour the clear PVA glue into a bowl.

2. Pour in 1 teaspoon (5 ml) each of diluted baking soda and contact lens solution.

3. Using your stirring utensil, mix the activator into the glue.

4. Repeat Steps 2 and 3 until the slime pulls away from the bowl. If the slime still looks too runny, alternate between adding a few drops of diluted baking soda and a few drops of contact lens solution until it thickens.

5. Knead the mixture with the stirring utensil or your hands.

6. Add drops of contact lens solution a little bit at a time until the slime is not sticky.

7. Enjoy your slime, and remember to store it in an airtight container when you're finished.

You can add stuff to the clear slime and still see it!

How to:
Make a Crystal-Clear Slime

• Wash and dry your bowl, stirring utensil, and hands before starting.

• Make sure your activator is clean and clear as well. Most liquid starches aren't clear, so use the activator made with diluted baking soda and contact lens solution (see page 11).

• Touch the slime as little as possible with your hands, especially if your hands are oily or dirty. Always make sure your hands are clean before playing with this slime to ensure it stays clear.

• Mix the ingredients slowly to minimize the amount of bubbles in the slime. Bubbles diminish the clarity of this slime.

• After completing the project, store the slime in an airtight container and let it sit for a few days for all the air bubbles to rise to the top and escape. If you leave it out under the sun or set it on a windowsill, it will become clearer faster, but it may melt. If it melts, pour a teaspoon of activator on top of the slime in the container and place it in a refrigerator or in front of air conditioning. Wait until the activator has fully soaked into the slime and enjoy!

Try this!

Avalanche Slime

Fill a clear container halfway with clear slime. Add a white PVA glue–based slime on top, close the lid, and wait three days for the white slime to drip down into the clear slime. It will make a cool avalanche effect!

Have a **SLIME** Party!

It's the perfect slime to share with a friend!

Matte Slime

This soft, spreadable slime is sometimes also called cream cheese slime. It's super-thick and dense, unlike butter slime, which is light and airy. It might look like something to put on a bagel, but remember: **Never eat it!**

WHAT YOU'LL NEED

Slime-Making Tool Kit

8 ounces (237 ml) white PVA glue

¾ cup (95 g) cornstarch or cornstarch-based baby powder

2 tablespoons (30 ml) lotion

¼ cup (60 ml) shaving cream

your choice of food coloring, pigment, or paint in any color

activator: 6 tablespoons (89 ml) liquid starch OR 3 teaspoons (15 ml) contact lens solution and 2 teaspoons (10 ml) diluted baking soda (see page 11)

WHAT YOU'LL DO

1. Pour the white PVA glue, cornstarch, lotion, shaving cream, and coloring ingredient into a bowl.

2. Using your stirring utensil, mix these ingredients together.

3. Pour in 1 tablespoon (15 ml) of liquid starch or 1 teaspoon (5 ml) each of diluted baking soda and contact lens solution.

4. Using your stirring utensil, mix the activator into the ingredients.

5. Repeat Steps 3 and 4 until the slime pulls away from the bowl. If the slime still looks too runny, try adding a few more drops of liquid starch, or alternate between adding a few drops of diluted baking soda and a few drops of contact lens solution until it thickens.

6. Knead the mixture with either the stirring utensil or your hands.

7. Add drops of liquid starch or contact lens solution a little bit at a time until the slime is not sticky. The slime should feel dense, stretchy, and soft.

8. Enjoy your slime, and remember to store it in an airtight container when you're finished.

Tip

If the slime is too thin, add more cornstarch! It may become stickier, so have your activator on hand. If it's too thick, run it under hot water a few times or add lotion.

Butter Slime

This very airy and light slime is mixed with soft clay. It can be spread like butter. Try it with a butter knife, but don't forget that **it's not for eating**!

WHAT YOU'LL NEED

Slime-Making Tool Kit

4 ounces (118 ml) white PVA glue

your choice of food coloring, pigment, or paint in any color

activator: 6 tablespoons (89 ml) liquid starch OR 3 teaspoons (15 ml) contact lens solution and 2 teaspoons (10 ml) diluted baking soda

8 ounces (227 g) modeling clay

2 tablespoons (30 ml) lotion

Tips

- Be sure to use **modeling clay** and **not earth clay**. Earth clay is used for pottery and won't produce a butter slime.

- You can change the color of your slime by using different colors of clay, too.

WHAT YOU'LL DO

1. Pour the white PVA glue and coloring ingredient into a bowl.

2. Pour in 1 tablespoon (15 ml) of liquid starch or 1 teaspoon (5 ml) each of diluted baking soda and contact lens solution. Using your stirring utensil, mix the ingredients.

3. Repeat Step 2 until the slime pulls away from the bowl. Knead the mixture with either the stirring utensil or your hands. If the slime still looks too runny, try adding a few more drops of liquid starch, or alternate between adding a few drops of diluted baking soda and a few drops of contact lens solution until it thickens.

4. Add drops of liquid starch or contact lens solution a little bit at a time until the slime is slightly sticky. The slight stickiness stops the clay from hardening the slime.

5. On a separate work surface, pour the lotion onto the modeling clay. Use your hands to knead the lotion into the clay.

6. Add the modeling clay and lotion mixture into the bowl of slime and knead everything together. The slime should feel soft and clay-like. If it's too hard, add in lotion 1 teaspoon (5 ml) at a time until it feels soft enough for your preference.

7. Enjoy your slime, and remember to store it in an airtight container when you're finished.

No-Glue
Butter Slime

Try this!

WHAT YOU'LL NEED

8 ounces (227 g) modeling clay

2 tablespoons (30 ml) lotion

WHAT YOU'LL DO

1. Referencing the instructions for Butter Slime, skip Steps 1 through 5.

2. Follow Step 6. Without the glue, it should feel slightly softer and more like the texture of the clay.

3. Add drops of the coloring ingredient into the slime.

4. Enjoy your slime, and remember to store it in an airtight container when you're finished.

Make fun shapes and cool designs!

Snowball Slime

This crunchy clear PVA glue–based slime looks and holds its shape just like snow.

WHAT YOU'LL NEED

Slime-Making Tool Kit

4 ounces (118 ml) clear PVA glue

activator: 6 tablespoons (89 ml) liquid starch OR 5 teaspoons (25 ml) contact lens solution and 4 teaspoons (20 ml) diluted baking soda

bowl (separate from what's in your usual Tool Kit)

1 cup (236 g) fake snow powder

Tip

Snowball slimes can pick up dust and dirt easily. To make sure your slime stays clean, always wash your hands before you play with it. After playing, put it back in its container with the lid on. If you leave it exposed, it will collect dust and become dirty.

WHAT YOU'LL DO

1. Pour the clear PVA glue into a bowl.

2. Pour in 1 tablespoon (15 ml) of liquid starch or 1 teaspoon (5 ml) each of diluted baking soda and contact lens solution.

3. Using your stirring utensil, mix the activator into the glue.

4. Repeat Steps 2 and 3 until the slime pulls away from bowl. The slime should be slightly sticky to hold in the fake snow. If the slime still looks too runny, try adding a few more drops of liquid starch, or alternate between adding a few drops of diluted baking soda and a few drops of contact lens solution until it thickens.

5. Knead the mixture until the activator is fully combined into the slime.

6. Pour the fake snow powder into a second bowl.

7. Dip the slime in the bowl of fake snow to get the fake snow to stick to the slime. Knead the slime to mix in the snow.

8. Repeat Step 7 as many times as you want. The more fake snow you mix into the slime, the crunchier the slime will be. Use a maximum ratio of 3 parts fake snow powder to 1 part slime; otherwise the snow may fall out.

9. Enjoy your slime, and remember to store it in an airtight container when you're finished.

Galaxy Slime

This pretty, multicolored slime resembles a galaxy with its small glitter "stars." Hold the universe in the palm of your hand.

WHAT YOU'LL NEED

Slime-Making Tool Kit

8 ounces (237 ml) white PVA glue

1 tablespoon (15 ml) lotion

activator: 6 tablespoons (89 ml) liquid starch OR 3 teaspoons (15 ml) contact lens solution and 2 teaspoons (10 ml) diluted baking soda

your choice of food coloring, pigment, or paint in blue and purple

glitter (silver, gold, blue, and purple glitter look best)

WHAT YOU'LL DO

1. Pour the white PVA glue and lotion into a bowl. Using your stirring utensil, mix these ingredients together.

2. Pour in 1 tablespoon (15 ml) of liquid starch or 1 teaspoon (5 ml) each of diluted baking soda and contact lens solution. Using your stirring utensil, mix the activator into the ingredients. Repeat this step until the slime pulls away from the bowl. If the slime still looks too runny, try adding a few more drops of liquid starch, or alternate between adding a few drops of diluted baking soda and a few drops of contact lens solution until it thickens.

3. Knead the mixture with either the stirring utensil or your hands.

4. Add drops of liquid starch or contact lens solution a little bit at a time until the slime is not sticky. The slime should feel slippery, soft, and stretchy and should not stick to your fingers.

5. Working on a clean surface, divide the slime into two equal halves. Pour the blue coloring ingredient onto one half of the slime and pour the purple coloring ingredient onto the other half of the slime. If you have a basic 4-color food coloring set, mix the red and blue dyes together to make purple.

6. Knead the blue and the purple slimes separately, using a stirring utensil, until the color is fully combined with the slime.

7. Combine the blue and purple slimes in your hands and swirl them together to marble. (See page 35 for details on how to create marbled slime.)

8. Place the marbled slime back in the bowl and sprinkle glitter over it. You can just leave the glitter on top of the slime, because when you mix them together, you might not be able to see the glitter. Add as much glitter as you want, but make sure not to put more than 1 ounce of glitter for every 3 ounces of slime, or the glitter may fall out.

9. Enjoy your slime, and remember to store it in an airtight container when you're finished.

How to: Marble Slime

To make marbled slime, hold all the different colored slimes in one hand, stretch the slimes, fold them, and repeat until there are different stripes of color running throughout the slime. Place it into a bowl and enjoy the marbled effect. See page 35 for how-to photos.

Tip

A fast and easy method of crushing water beads is to put them in a blender with water at a ratio of 2 teaspoons (10 ml) of water to every 1 cup (237 g) of presoaked water beads. **Watch out for the sharp blades, and ask an adult for help using the blender.** Depending on the strength of your blender, it usually takes about 30 seconds to 1 minute to crush all the beads until there are no big chunks remaining. If you don't have a blender, the sandwich-bag method (used in the Bubble-Bath Slime project) works just fine!

Bubble-Bath Slime

Bubble-Bath Slime is a jiggly clear slime that looks like a warm bubble bath. This slime requires advance planning because it will take about a day for your water beads to soak.

WHAT YOU'LL NEED

Slime-Making Tool Kit

¼ teaspoon (1 g) dry water beads

zippered sandwich bag

8 ounces (237 ml) clear PVA glue

bowl (separate from what's in your usual Tool Kit)

water

activator: 6 tablespoons (89 ml) liquid starch OR 5 teaspoons (25 ml) contact lens solution and 4 teaspoons (20 ml) diluted baking soda (see page 11)

your choice of food coloring, pigment, or paint (optional)

WARNING:

This slime uses water beads, which pose a potential choking hazard. Make sure an adult is supervising!

WHAT YOU'LL DO

1. Place the dry beads into a bowl with the water. Once they soak up the water, you should have about 1 cup (237 g) of beads. It will take about a day for the water to absorb.

2. Place the water beads in a zippered sandwich bag and, using your fingers, break the water beads apart until they are completely crushed with no big chunks.

3. Pour the clear PVA glue and the crushed water beads into a bowl. Using your stirring utensil, mix these ingredients together.

4. Pour in 1 tablespoon (15 ml) of liquid starch or 1 teaspoon (5 ml) each of diluted baking soda and contact lens solution. Using your stirring utensil, mix the activator into the ingredients.

5. Repeat Step 4 until the slime pulls away from bowl. If the slime still looks too runny, try adding a few more drops of liquid starch, or alternate between adding a few drops of diluted baking soda and a few drops of contact lens solution until it thickens.

6. Pour in your coloring ingredient, if using.

7. Knead the slime with either the stirring utensil or your hands.

8. Add drops of liquid starch or contact lens solution a little bit at a time until the slime is not sticky. The slime should feel jiggly and textured.

9. Enjoy your slime, and remember to store it in an airtight container when you're finished.

Tip

There are different types of beads you can use for foam slime. You can use the beads in beanbags and neck pillows or regular craft beads. Experiment for different kinds of crunch!

ROARRRR!

Foam Slime

This crunchy slime is full of foam beads that pop each time you pull, mash, twist, and poke it.

WHAT YOU'LL NEED

Slime-Making Tool Kit

4 ounces (118 ml) clear PVA glue

your choice of food coloring, pigment, or paint in any color

activator: 6 tablespoons (89 ml) liquid starch OR 5 teaspoons (25 ml) contact lens solution and 4 teaspoons (20 ml) diluted baking soda (see page 11)

bowl (separate from what's in your usual Tool Kit)

1 cup (236 g) craft foam beads

WARNING

This slime uses craft foam beads, which pose a potential choking hazard. Make sure an adult is supervising!

WHAT YOU'LL DO

1. Pour the clear PVA glue and coloring ingredient into a bowl.

2. Pour in 1 tablespoon (15 ml) of liquid starch or 1 teaspoon (5 ml) each of diluted baking soda and contact lens solution. Using your stirring utensil, mix the activator into the ingredients.

3. Repeat Step 2 until the slime pulls away from the bowl. The slime should be a little sticky so that it holds in the craft foam beads. If the slime still looks too runny, try adding a few more drops of liquid starch, or alternate between adding a few drops of diluted baking soda and a few drops of contact lens solution until it thickens.

4. Knead the mixture with either the stirring utensil or your hands until the activator is fully combined into the slime.

5. Pour craft foam beads into a second bowl.

6. Dip the slime in the craft foam beads to get the beads to stick to the slime. Knead the slime to mix the beads in.

7. Repeat Step 7 as many times as you want. The more beads you mix into the slime, the crunchier the slime will be. Be careful to not add too many beads. Use a maximum ratio of 3 parts craft foam beads to 1 part slime; otherwise, the beads may fall out.

8. Enjoy your slime, and remember to store it in an airtight container when you're finished.

Bubbly Slime

This slime takes a few days to create, but the wait will be worth it for that satisfying *crunch, sizzle,* and *pop!*

WHAT YOU'LL NEED

Slime-Making Tool Kit

8 ounces (237 ml) white PVA glue

4 ounces (118 ml) shaving cream

2 tablespoons (30 ml) lotion

your choice of food coloring or paint in any color

6 pumps foaming hand soap

3 pumps foaming face wash (optional)

activator: 6 tablespoons (89 ml) liquid starch OR 3 teaspoons (15 ml) contact lens solution and 2 teaspoons (10 ml) diluted baking soda (see page 11)

WHAT YOU'LL DO

1. Pour the white PVA glue, shaving cream, lotion, and coloring ingredient into a bowl. Pump the foaming hand soap and (optional) foaming face wash into the same bowl.

2. Using your stirring utensil, mix these ingredients together.

3. Pour in 1 tablespoon (15 ml) of liquid starch or 1 teaspoon (5 ml) each of diluted baking soda and contact lens solution.

4. Using your stirring utensil, mix the activator into the ingredients.

5. Repeat Steps 3 and 4 until the slime pulls away from the bowl. If the slime still looks too runny, try adding a few more drops of liquid starch, or alternate between adding a few drops of diluted baking soda and a few drops of contact lens solution until it thickens.

6. Knead the mixture with either the stirring utensil or your hands.

7. Add drops of liquid starch or contact lens solution a little bit at a time until the slime is not sticky.

8. Place the slime in an airtight container and let it sit for at least 3 days for the bubbles to form.

9. When the slime has an abundance of small bubbles on the top, it is ready. When you play with it, the slime will make a sizzling sound, which is the sound of the bubbles popping.

Before

After

Tips

- The more foaming hand soap you use, the more bubbles you'll have in the slime. However, do not use more than 3 times the amount of glue or the slime may be hard to hold.

- Foaming face wash makes the slime fluffier, but doesn't add many bubbles to the slime.

How to:
Soften Your Slime

Bubbly Slime will harden the more you play with it. After two or three play sessions, the bubbles will deflate and you will end up with a hard slime. To soften it, you can run it under hot water or add lotion. If you want to reactivate the bubbles, add more foaming hand soap and wait another 3 days.

Iceberg Slime

Try this!

Leave your bubbly slime in a container with no lid for 4 days, and it will turn into a crunchy, fizzy slime!

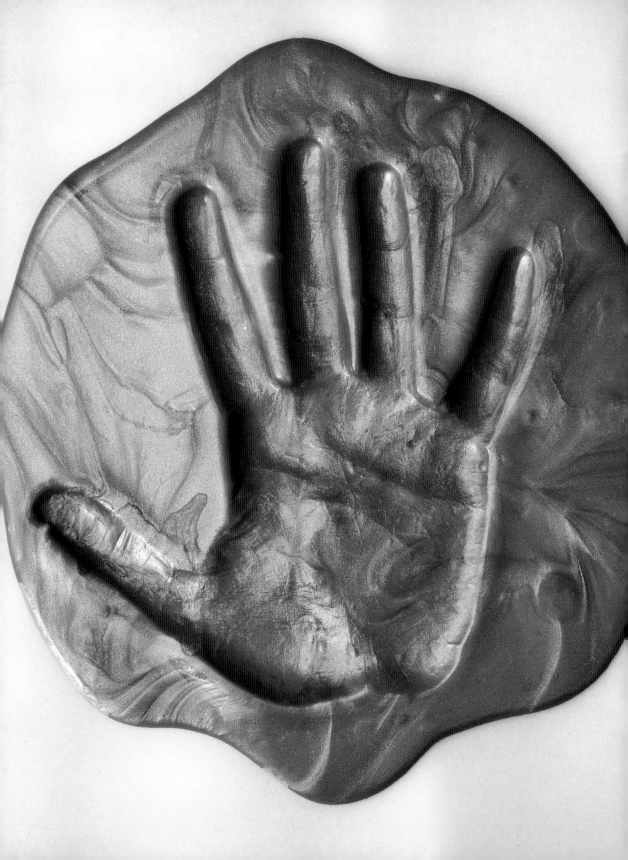

Metallic Slime

When you squeeze, poke, and pull this super-metallic slime, the pigments catch the light and create a shimmery, shiny effect.

WHAT YOU'LL NEED

Slime-Making Tool Kit

8 ounces (237 ml) clear PVA glue

1 tablespoon (15 ml) metallic paint or 1 teaspoon (4 g) metallic pigment powder in any color

activator: 6 tablespoons (89 ml) liquid starch OR 5 teaspoons (25 ml) contact lens solution and 4 teaspoons (20 ml) diluted baking soda (see page 11)

Tip

If you want to make a variety of colored metallic slimes, just get a white pearl pigment or paint and add food coloring to it! You can make a rainbow of metallic colors with a white pearl pigment or paint, and you'll also save money in the long run.

WHAT YOU'LL DO

1. Pour the clear PVA glue and metallic paint or powder into a bowl.

2. Using your stirring utensil, mix these ingredients together.

3. Pour in 1 tablespoon (15 ml) of liquid starch or 1 teaspoon (5 ml) each of diluted baking soda and contact lens solution.

4. Using your stirring utensil, mix the activator into the ingredients.

5. Repeat Steps 3 and 4 until the slime pulls away from the bowl. If the slime still looks too runny, try adding a few more drops of liquid starch, or alternate between adding a few drops of diluted baking soda and a few drops of contact lens solution until it thickens.

6. Knead the slime with the stirring utensil or your hands.

7. Add drops of liquid starch or contact lens solution a little bit at a time until the slime is not sticky. The slime should feel soft, stretchy, and not sticky.

8. Enjoy your slime, and remember to store it in an airtight container when you're finished.

Papier-Mâché Slime

This thick, chunky slime looks kind of like the stuff you use for art projects.

WHAT YOU'LL NEED

Slime-Making Tool Kit

8 ounces (237 ml) white PVA glue

1 tablespoon (15 ml) lotion

your choice of food coloring or paint in any color

activator: 6 tablespoons (89 ml) liquid starch OR 3 teaspoons (15 ml) contact lens solution and 2 teaspoons (10 ml) diluted baking soda (see page 11)

3–4 tissues

Tip

Try kneading the slime until there are no clumps. This creates a putty-like slime that can be spread like a butter slime!

WHAT YOU'LL DO

1. Pour the white PVA glue, lotion, and coloring ingredient into a bowl. Using your stirring utensil, mix these ingredients together.

2. Pour in 1 tablespoon (15 ml) of liquid starch or 1 teaspoon (5 ml) each of diluted baking soda and contact lens solution. Using your stirring utensil, mix the activator into the ingredients. Repeat this step until the slime pulls away from the bowl. If the slime still looks too runny, try adding a few more drops of liquid starch, or alternate between adding a few drops of diluted baking soda and a few drop of contact lens solution until it thickens.

3. Knead the mixture with either the stirring utensil or your hands.

4. Add drops of liquid starch or contact lens solution a little bit at a time until the slime is not sticky. The slime should feel slippery, soft, and stretchy and should not stick to your fingers.

5. Tear the tissues into small pieces and add to your slime. Knead the slime to fully combine the tissues with the slime. The slime should be smooth with very few clumps.

6. Add more tissues until you're satisfied with the texture. The more tissues you add, the thicker and clumpier the slime will be.

7. Enjoy your slime, and remember to store it in an airtight container when you're finished.

Fluffy Slime

This slime is soft, light, and fluffy. It has a matte appearance at first, but it can deflate and turn into a regular glossy slime later.

WHAT YOU'LL NEED

Slime-Making Tool Kit

8 ounces (237 ml) white PVA glue

4 ounces (118 ml) shaving cream

2 tablespoons (30 ml) lotion

your choice of food coloring, pigment, or paint in any color

3 pumps foaming hand soap

3 pumps foaming face wash (optional)

activator: 6 tablespoons (89 ml) liquid starch OR 3 teaspoons (15 ml) contact lens solution and 2 teaspoons (10 ml) diluted baking soda (see page 11)

WHAT YOU'LL DO

1. Pour the white PVA glue, shaving cream, lotion, and coloring ingredient into a bowl. Pump the foaming hand soap and foaming face wash, if using, into the same bowl.

2. Using your stirring utensil, mix these ingredients together.

3. Pour in 1 tablespoon (15 ml) of liquid starch or 1 teaspoon (5 ml) each of diluted baking soda and contact lens solution.

4. Using your stirring utensil, mix the activator into the ingredients.

5. Repeat Steps 3 and 4 until the slime pulls away from the bowl. If the slime still looks too runny, try adding a few more drops of liquid starch, or alternate between adding a few drops of diluted baking soda and a few drops of contact lens solution until it thickens.

6. Knead the mixture with either the stirring utensil or your hands.

7. Add drops of liquid starch or contact lens solution a little bit at a time until the slime is not sticky. The slime should feel soft, airy, and stretchy.

8. Enjoy your slime, and remember to store it in an airtight container when you're finished.

Tips

• If you add foaming face wash when making your slime, the fluffy slime can self-inflate! After you add the face wash, just play with the slime and swirl it a few times; it should start to grow. Make sure you use a large bowl!

• If your fluffy slime has deflated, add some more shaving cream to bring it back to its original fluffy form. Unfortunately, deflation is inevitable, but you can always reinflate your slime to preserve it.

• If the slime has hardened, that means it may be too old to play with. Simply add some water or lotion, and it should be good as new!

Find things around the
house to mold your
slime onto!

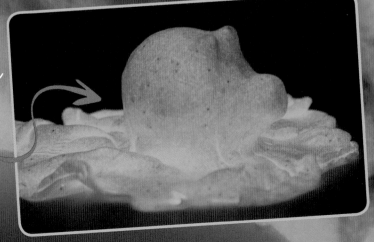

Glow-in-the-Dark Slime

This looks like an ordinary slime in the daylight, but turn off the lights and it will glow in the dark!

WHAT YOU'LL NEED

Slime-Making Tool Kit

8 ounces (237 ml) clear PVA glue

1 teaspoon (4 g) glow-in-the-dark powder

activator: 6 tablespoons (89 ml) liquid starch OR 5 teaspoons (25 ml) contact lens solution and 4 teaspoons (20 ml) diluted baking soda (see page 11)

Tip

Glow-in-the-dark powder, also known as phosphorescent powder, needs to be "charged" with light before it can glow in the dark. Leave your slime under sunlight or another light source for a few minutes before turning out the lights to watch it glow. The longer you let the slime charge, the brighter it will glow.

WHAT YOU'LL DO

1. Pour the clear PVA glue and glow-in-the-dark powder into a bowl.

2. Using your stirring utensil, mix these ingredients together.

3. Pour in 1 tablespoon (15 ml) of liquid starch or 1 teaspoon (5 ml) each of diluted baking soda and contact lens solution.

4. Using your stirring utensil, mix the activator into the ingredients.

5. Repeat Steps 3 and 4 until the slime pulls away from the bowl. If the slime still looks too runny, try adding a few more drops of liquid starch, or alternate between adding a few drops of diluted baking soda and a few drops of contact lens solution until it thickens.

6. Knead the mixture with either the stirring utensil or your hands.

7. Add drops of liquid starch or contact lens solution a little bit at a time until the slime is not sticky. The slime should feel soft and stretchy.

8. Enjoy your slime, and remember to store it in an airtight container when you're finished.

Resources

Big craft stores will have a majority of the materials you need, like PVA glue, modeling clay, glitter, metallic and glow-in-the-dark paints, metallic pigments, vase fillers, and craft foam beads.

- Michaels (michaels.com)
- A.C. Moore (acmoore.com)
- Hobby Lobby (hobbylobby.com)

PAINT AND PIGMENTS:

- Dick Blick Art Materials (dickblick.com)
- Pearls and Pigments (pearlsandpigments.com)

GLOW-IN-THE-DARK POWDER:

- Cool Glow (coolglow.com)
- Solar Color Dust (solarcolordust.com)

WATER BEADS AND FAKE SNOW POWDER:

- Walmart (walmart.com)
- Hobby Chimp (hobbychimp.com)

PVA glue is widely available, but another resource outside of craft retailers is office-supply stores. Packing peanuts can also be found at these stores.

Acknowledgments

Thank you to my mom, who has painfully overlooked the multiple times when I've dropped slime on the carpet. I also want to thank all my followers on Instagram who support me! Finally, thanks to my friends—Min, for giving me that boost when I was just beginning my account; Audrey, Emily, Lianna, and Angela, for being people I can confide in always; and my friends in real life who I can laugh with always.

Hi! My name is Selina, and I'm from Northern California. I love drawing, reading, and playing the piano, ukulele, and guitar. I run an account dedicated to slime on Instagram (@anathemaslime), and I have a slime shop at anathemaslime.com. My favorite slimes to make are thick fluffy slimes, or crunchy foam slimes.

Image Credits

Project and people photography by Christopher Bain.

iStock.com: ©4kodiak (glass measuring cup-2); ©aimy27feb (clear liquid bowl); ©Akinshin (blue bubbles, sparce); ©ambassador806 (multicolor starbursts); ©AnnaSqBerg (color speech bubbles); ©arkady2013 (clear balls/detail); ©artJazz (green powder explosion); ©Barcin (heart in snow); ©Bellanatella (multicolor clay spots); ©Larisa Bozhikova (white cream); ©Bsiro (white foam dollop); ©cclickclick (snow, heart-shaped glitter frame); ©Chaluk (gold/black glitter); ©Galina Cherryka (directional arrows); ©CLFortin (multicolor sprinkles-right side); ©clubfoot (plastic measuring spoons); ©Cometary (white slime detail); ©CPaulussen (gold stars); ©Delpixart (multicolor border); ©Larysa Dodz (white containers); ©EHStock (mixing bowls); ©Enviromantic (white board background); ©Eskaylim (wood spoon & powder, blue utensils); ©flas100 (blue splatter); ©Flyfloor (spoon); ©Richard Galbraith (POP burst); ©David Goh (multiple design elements); ©hiro-k 9 (gold/silver dots); ©Judit Hoffmann (sand-flat); ©Ideas Studio (abstract explosions); ©Imperasiusy (multicolor watercolor splashes); ©Ivymany (color tech dots); ©joto (beer bubbles); ©Naoki Kim (white crumpled paper); ©Wojciech Kozielczyk (paint bottles); ©Krafla (transparent drip); ©LoveTheWind (foam on white); ©Mattjeacock (silver stars); ©Nik Merkulov (white shaving foam); ©Milkos (gold glitter sand); ©NaCreative (blue bubbles/crowded); ©naqiewei (circular polka dots); ©Nerthuz (white bottle); ©Don Nichols (plastic peanuts); ©nu1983 (talcum powder); ©Obewon (clear glass bottle); ©ONYXprj (science symbols, magic symbols/unicorns); ©Pavlinec (pouring milk); ©Pepifoto (soap & sponges, pile of sand); ©Photosbyjam (food coloring); ©Phuchit (white polymer balls); ©Pingebat (rainbow fireworks); ©Pixelliebe (multicolor confetti); ©PLAINVIEW (shiny powder); ©robynmac (multicolor sprinkles); ©Rgbdigital (white candle/glass); ©Samohin (orange splatter); ©Scvos (gold glitter); ©showcake (white container/orange cap); ©Somnath_DC (dye powders); ©Speakman Photography (wax drips); ©Mary Stocker (pop art UFO badges); ©Subjug (tissue box); ©Sussenn (speech bubble); ©TopStockFoto (foam on hand); ©Wacomka (white glue splatter); ©WEKWEK (glitter varnish circles); ©Wwing (food coloring/red spilled); ©Polyudova Yulia (comic fish); ©Zhemchuzhina (pink comic splatter)

Index

Note: Page numbers in *italics* indicate projects.

The End!